The Thinner Blue Line

The Thinner Blue Line

THE LIFE OF A FEMALE METROPOLITAN POLICE OFFICER

SOPHIE A. MATTHEWS

authorHOUSE®

AuthorHouse™ UK
1663 Liberty Drive
Bloomington, IN 47403 USA
www.authorhouse.co.uk
Phone: 0800.197.4150

Published by AuthorHouse 11/27/2014

ISBN: 978-1-4969-8924-6 (sc)
ISBN: 978-1-4969-8928-4 (e)

The police are the public
and the public are the police;
the police being only members of the public
who are paid to give full time attention
to duties which are incumbent on every
citizen in the interests of community
welfare and existence.
Sir Robert Peel – 1788-1850.

Contents

Introduction xi

Chapter 1.   I Didn't Always Want To
              Be A Police Officer 1
Chapter 2.   How Did It All Happen? 5
Chapter 3.   London Calling 11
Chapter 4.   In Uniform 21
Chapter 5.   Frontline 25
Chapter 6.   CID 31
Chapter 7.   Murder Most Horrid –
              The Homicide Squad 41
Chapter 8.   Blood And Gore 57
Chapter 9.   The Old Bailey 67
Chapter 10.   Women In The Work Place &
              Sexism? 75
Chapter 11.   Public Perception 81
Chapter 12.   Home-Life & Family 91
Chapter 13.   A Mothers Pride 95

Chapter 14.   Nasty Surprises.................................. 99

Chapter 15.   7/7 107

Chapter 16.   The Future 111

Chapter 17.   I Didn't Always Want To
              Be A Police Officer 113

Chapter 18.   A Final Note 117

Introduction

I have been a female police officer in the Metropolitan Police Service for a few years now and so decided to write this book. I have written it for the three following reasons:

Firstly, for my fellow police officers, who are out there every day giving their all, this book is for you. For you to both enjoy and relate to in a way that only those in "The Job" can.

Secondly, for the general public who may wish to read about the life of a police officer in the forever busy, often ugly and unforgiving Metropolis of London. It is not a 'nine to five' job and we can't just 'shut off' when we finish our shifts for the day. We are servants to the Queen and are on duty every minute of our lives, expected to respond and act accordingly at any time or any place. We are too often berated and crucified by the media but rarely praised or thanked for the everyday good that we do, and help we provide to others. We give our all, sacrificing our personal lives and relationships, only to be faced daily with the atrocities of life, most will never get to experience.

Finally, I also wrote this for those of you planning or even just contemplating joining the police. This book is an attempt to provide you with some eye-opening realities of what it can be like out there as a police officer in the thin blue line, and more specifically, as a female police officer, in the thinner blue line.

Chapter 1

I Didn't Always Want To Be A Police Officer

I didn't always want be a police officer.

But what a life so far.....

In my service I have wrapped up dead bodies, searched the most horrific crime scenes and convicted killers at The Old Bailey.

I have arrested numerous offenders ranging from shop-lifters to murderers.

I have had lengthy foot-chases and high-speed vehicle pursuits.

I have been slapped, bitten, spat at and wrestled to the ground.

I have appeared on Crimewatch during a live televised appeal, and also interviewed by the BBC for a police documentary.

I have helped advise a Hollywood actress research her role as a police officer.

I have met the best of mankind but also the worst.

I have seen things the general public will never have the pleasure, or the horror of experiencing.

Being a police officer has brought out the best of my character but also the worst.

There are terrible images in my head which will never be erased.

I have sacrificed a marriage, possibly the chance of having children, and friendships with those who don't understand the life I lead and the hours I work.

I ask myself sometimes why I bother doing what I do.

Why don't I get a normal 'nine to five' job like most people?

My life simply is 'The Job'.

So after eleven years service & many more to go, I ask myself...

Would I do it all again?....

CHAPTER 2

How Did It All Happen?

I didn't always want to be a police officer.

Many officers, if you ask them, will say it was lifelong dream of theirs and joining the police is all they ever wanted to do since childhood.

This wasn't so in my case. My dream as a young girl was to work in the world of forensic science. Don't get me wrong growing up in the 80's I spent many evenings in with my dad watching 'cop shows' like, Dempsey & Makepeace, Hill Street Blues, The Bill and Cagney & Lacey. My dad had a big 'thing' for Sharon Gless playing the feisty Christine Cagney so we never missed an episode. I loved her hard, but charismatic character too. He used to say that he could see me one day doing what she did. I would entertain the idea in my head until the show finished...and then I would imagine doing something else, like working with animals, or journalism, but mostly forensic science.

In my later teens I loved the Die Hard and Lethal Weapon films which I watched over and over again. To me Detective John McClain & Martin Riggs were simply awesome. I think these police shows and films planted a seed in the back of my head where it remained for many years.

So I followed my dream of forensic science and after finishing college I left for London to study a Bsc Degree in Biological Sciences. After graduation, I stayed on in London and within a couple of months I began working as a civilian fingerprint technician at New Scotland Yard (NSY).

This was my first job in 'The Met' (Metropolitan Police Service) and, not that I knew it then, it paved the way for a long and diverse career in criminal investigation.

I was trained to compare fingerprint marks through ridge detail and patterns. I was still working there in 2000 when' Livescan' also known as 'NAFIS' (National Automated Fingerprint Identification System) was introduced into the Met. This was developed in the USA and meant police officers could now scan fingerprints of those arrested instead of inking them the old fashioned way.

I loved my time at NSY in fingerprints (called SO4 back then) but after two years I believed my big break had come along at the Forensic Science Service (FSS) laboratory in Lambeth, London. The position of an assistant forensic scientist opened up and I thought that this was the start of a life-long career the day I got accepted for the job.

That was the start of 2001 and that year stands out to me but not for the reasons that I thought it would. That was the year the Twin Towers were flown into. That was the year I joined the FSS but by September I had already decided to quit.

Forensics was nothing at all like what I expected it to be. I found it to be so dull & monotonous, a far cry from the glamorous and exciting world I had always envisaged. I spent the majority of my days staring down a microscope for hours and hours looking for minute traces of blood on clothing or weapons. If I was lucky enough to not be doing that I was instead taping exhibits from crime scenes, victims or suspects for traces of hairs & fibres. It was pretty much the same thing day in, day out.

The forensic procedure I used for each case was generally always the same. However the case facts in the police files which came into the laboratory with each submission were always different and far more interesting than at my end of the deal. I found myself wishing I was investigating these cases and I was quite envious of the police officers out there amongst it all, not stuck in a window-less laboratory day in day out doing the same old, same old.

Funnily enough it was this major and unexpected disappointment of my now fading career in forensic science which got me back to thinking about that planted seed from many years back.

Just days before 9/11 rocked the world I handed in my notice at the FSS and decided to take time out overseas and to also seriously reconsider my future career options. Just a few days after the planes were high-jacked in the skies over the USA, I myself caught a plane and flew the long trek over to Australia.

I travelled and worked along the eastern coast from Melbourne up to Brisbane doing simple jobs in shops, in a casino and also at Sea World on the Gold Coast. Whilst out there the seed in my mind grew, and so I decided to do the inevitable upon my return back to London and apply to the Metropolitan Police Service……. this time as a police officer.

CHAPTER 3

London Calling

Getting into the Metropolitan Police Service was fairly simple and quick when I applied in 2002. At that time it was recruiting in big drives to get the numbers of officers up across London. They were specifically appealing for more women and ethnic minorities to apply. This was the ideal time to submit my interest.

After being successfully paper sifted through the initial application form phase I was invited to Hendon training school in North London for an interview and assessment day. This consisted of basic English and Maths exams, an observational video test, a physical exercise assessment and a formal interview.

The physical assessment was pointless and a bit of a joke in my opinion. It consisted of a bleep test at a very low level, a push-pull test for the upper body strength and a grip test to test the forearm strength.

The bleep test is a shuttle run test during which you have to run from one end of the gym to the other within the specific time. After each stretch the time of the bleep gets quicker so effectively you begin the test at a walk then build up to a jog and then a run. Each stretch was counted as 0.1, so after ten stretches of the gym you had run 1.0.

When I did the bleep test in 2002 it was set at the pass level of 8.1 for women. The men's pass level was slightly higher. I passed the bleep test fairly easily. By the next year the women's bleep test pass mark was lowered. Rumour had it that this was because too many women were failing it. So it was lowered from level 8.1 to level 5.4 to pass the majority of women. I don't understand the logic in lowering it. What is the point in even having the bleep test incorporated into the physical assessment at all, if the aim is to pass those who can't run faster than a jog? How is that safe? helpful to anyone? or practical during a foot chase?

If anyone reading has this tried the bleep test you will understand my point of view. If you cannot reach at least level 8.1 you are simply not fit enough to be a police officer.

I recall in later years after that bleep test during an OST class (Officer Safety Training) the instructor telling us that we need to make it a priority and take it upon ourselves to stay fit. He said it was one thing to have the ability to run fast enough to catch the bad guys you will be chasing, but it is far more important to be fit enough to run AWAY from a gang of angry youths who want to beat you to a pulp, or from the knife-wielding maniac who wants to take your head off! I totally agreed with him, and that advice has always stayed with me.

I passed the entrance exams (including the physical assessment – surprise, surprise) and in 2003 began my first day at Hendon training school as a new police recruit.

On my first day I admit that I was still unsure if I had done the right thing.

That was until the whole intake of recruits (a few hundred of us) was piled into the lecture theatre and shown a video. With the backing track 'London

Calling' by The Clash blasting out, we watched footage of the Met's finest in action during the Brixton riots, the poll tax riots, the miners strikes & other famous scenes involving the Metropolitan Police. It sent a chill right through me & I thought "this is it!" To this day that song pumps me up and makes me feel good when I'm tired or when I've had a particularly bad day. All the pride and excitement of being a police officer comes flooding back when I remember scenes from that video from years ago.

Training at the Peel Centre at Hendon consisted of eighteen weeks. Training was residential back then and I lived in the one of the two huge ugly tower blocks on the estate. One tower block was designated for the female recruits and the other for the male recruits. We were banned from going into the other respective tower block, but as you can imagine rules are there to be broken.

A typical day's training involved acting out role plays, attending classes, sitting exams, marching drills and physical exercise classes.

The morning parades took place at the start of everyday before class. They were very formal and disliked by all. We all had to line up in our respective classes and were inspected from head to toe by an officer of rank. Our uniform was expected to be freshly ironed, free of any lint or fluff and boots were to be shined to a high standard. The officer would walk amongst the recruits and pull out any one who didn't come up to scratch, and even the odd one who was up to scratch but keeping people on their toes was the name of the game. I was lucky enough never to get pulled out. Those who did were made to stand out at the front of the rest of the parade the following morning and were inspected again. It was an embarrassment. I always hated those parades.

The evenings involved a fair bit of drinking. The Claddagh Ring public house, situated off-campus was the place to be on a Sunday night. Most recruits had returned from their weekend visits back home that evening and most of us got quite merry before the next week's classes and exams began.

The 'Peel Bar' was located within the training school grounds and was often frequented during the week.

These evenings of drink at Hendon, for the most, were a taste of what was to come - the big drinking culture, which is and always has been so prevalent in The Met.

You can often spot a well seasoned detective by his whiskey tinted rose cheeks and rounded beer belly.

Fitness however was also encouraged. Hendon stills boasts it's athletics track which I used to train on frequently. There were also squash courts and a gym and both were often occupied by the fitter recruits. It was a very warm summer, which was used to our advantage as some of us often lay out studying on the grass in the sunshine between classes, whilst the lads played football.

I loved my days at Hendon. I think probably because I went to university I found the studying and the exams fairly easy. Others did not. Every Friday we sat written exams on the subjects taught that previous week. If a recruit failed a certain number of exams they were back-classed or worse still, sent home.

The subjects taught covered many aspects of policing and London life. We were taught about criminal offences, reporting and recording crime, arresting offenders, custody practices and the court systems, alongside religion, culture, diversity and much more.

We were also examined on practical role plays which were quite daunting. We would line up outside a building which inside housed several small rooms. Once inside the building we each waited outside our designated room until a buzzer sounded. We were then to each enter our own room not knowing what incident we would face once inside. All we knew was that an examiner (a sergeant) was sat in a corner, and fellow recruits from other intakes acted out an incident that we then had two or three minutes to deal with. We were marked by the sergeant on our performances. The examination was also video recorded. I still have one of my tapes…cringe-worthy.

I remember the first role play session my class ever did. One of the girls in my sister class entered her designated room, and closed the door. Seconds later we all heard an almighty roar and big bangs followed by a scream. We then, seconds later, saw the same girl run out of the room screaming and crying followed by the stooge (a big built sergeant in this case) who was running after her with a baseball bat whilst yelling at the top of his voice. She fled the building and we didn't see her again for a short while. The rest of us just stood there in silence, stunned, and all thinking the same thing…"crap, I'm next".

The incidents we had to deal with were anything from traffic accidents, domestic situations, pub fights, arrests and physical injuries requiring medical assistance.

Some of the role play expectations were far-fetched and unfairly marked. A friend of mine was faced with a motorbike accident scenario and had to treat the injured rider on the floor. There was no actual motorbike in the room during this role play exercise, just the rider on the floor. Since the role play was inside a room, there was obviously no real road, no traffic to control, or real injuries to the 'victim'. Anyway my friend was failed on this scenario, even though he correctly dealt with the injuries, because he failed to go over to the motorbike (which wasn't actually there) to turn off the ignition!

These role play scenarios however many you do, will never prepare you for what you will actually be faced with on the street, I can honestly say fact is much stranger than fiction.

My class passed out on graduation day with just twelve of the original twenty recruits. The rest had failed and so were back-classed or sent home for good. All those who failed in my class were men. All the women passed. Was there a reason for this?....I honestly don't know.

I was happy after I finally graduated, but also sad as that was when everyone went their separate ways. Many of the recruits had naturally become quite close during those eighteen weeks and strong friendships had been forged.

After one week off to recuperate, we all started our new paths, posted to our various police stations across the thirty two boroughs of London, finally, as real police officers out in the real world.

Chapter 4

In Uniform

I began my two year phase as a probationary police officer on a borough in south London.

My first few weeks were spent on a 'street duties' team with about eight other recruits, a few experienced constables who were our tutors, and a sergeant who was in charge. Street duties was basically a short period of just a few weeks to give new officers a taste of 'real life' in the police before they get sent to a response team, by which time they would be patrolling the streets of London in a pair or sometimes, alone. Whilst on street duties we travelled around the borough in a mini bus and dealt with whatever came our way, mainly petty crime arrests, minor traffic offences and cordon controls at crime scenes.

My time on street duties was quite uneventful apart from one incident, which to this day, still baffles me and was one of those rare occasions I earlier spoke of when I was ashamed of being in the police.

We were on patrol one winter evening. It was dark, cold and pouring down with rain. The driver of our street duties mini-bus was an acting inspector (a sergeant acting up as the next rank). He stopped the bus as he noticed a big dark object in the middle of the road in front of us. We all got out and with a few others I approached this object in the road which we quickly realised was actually a woman curled up on the wet ground. She was soaked through and was shivering. I managed to get her up on her feet and over to a bench where I sat her down. She was clearly emotionally unstable and could not communicate with us. Because she was shivering so much I took off my police jacket and put it around her in an attempt to keep her warm. I could not believe what I then heard. The acting inspector asked me what right I had to put my police-issue jacket around this woman. He told me that we did not know what diseases she may have and that my jacket will now have to be destroyed. I had just ruined police property at a financial cost to the Met. My reply was pretty much this…. "The Met can bill me" What annoyed me furthermore was that he said this to me in ear-shot of this poor woman and the other probationers.

Policing is not just about knowing the law and arresting the bad guys. The most important piece of equipment any police officer has at his or her disposal is their voice, and how they choose to communicate with it. This woman was simply in need of help, reassurance, kind words and the gesture of an over-coat. The ambulance arrived moments later and took over her care. To this day the action by that senior officer, who was in a position of influence over us, still bothers me. I would do exactly the same thing again. I often wonder if he would too?

The only other moment which stands out to me from my street duties days was my first arrest. It was by no means an exciting arrest or the result of a shocking crime. It was the arrest of a seventeen year old girl for stealing a pair of socks. I cannot lie, I was very much underwhelmed at the time that this was to be my first arrest. However I had many, many more memorable and sometimes shocking arrests to come.

After successfully completing street duties I joined my response team and that is where the real frontline policing started.

CHAPTER 5

Frontline

I spent the majority of my time in uniform on a response team patrolling the streets, attending shoplifting calls, burglaries, drunken fights & domestic disputes.

My favourite calls though were 'suspects on' which were generally when burglars were thought to be still at the scene of a burglary. Such calls were often during the night and were mainly in people's homes. One of my funniest memories is during one of these calls. A member of the public had phoned 999 around 2am after noticing that the front door of a neighbouring house opposite was open and the house was in darkness. I and a male colleague arrived on scene and quietly entered the property. He went upstairs whilst I looked around the ground floor, my heart racing, hoping to catch a burglar off-guard. I suddenly heard a loud girly scream followed by a second girly scream coming from upstairs. I ran up the stairs, heart racing even faster, only to find my male colleague stood facing a woman sat upright in her bed, sheets held up against her chest and both of them still screaming in shock. She had simply left the door open after putting the bins out that night. She was fast asleep and had no idea police had entered the house until a torch was shone in her face. My colleague did not expect to find a woman upstairs sleeping in her bed when he shone his torch around the room. They had both scared the wits out of one another. I had to leave the room so neither of them saw me giggling.

Once in the middle of a night shift we were called to a school because the alarms were all going off. The school grounds were huge so we brought a police dog in and he sniffed out a young lad hiding under a car. His friends had made off and he was too scared to run away, so he attempted to hide. There was no way the dog was going to miss him under that car. Those police dogs are amazing. I remember once when I was in CID attending a fire scene inside a shop. It was the following day after the fire so it had long been extinguished by the brigade, so was by the morning a messy burnt out shell of ash, rubble and broken glass. We had no idea how or where the fire had started. The very eager and excited cocker spaniel, who was decked out in little booties to protect his paws from the glass (so cute), ran inside the shop and within seconds found the accelerant site which he indicated to his handler. The investigation went on to prove that the fire had been intentionally started by the owner who was later charged with insurance fraud and other offences.

I adore the police dogs. They love their work, as to them it's just a game, after which they get a treat. Their handlers adore them too and it is lovely to see them at work together. The handlers are both very protective and proud of their partners, and so they should be. Generally speaking if there is something there for them to find, the highly trained canine will find it.

I have used several types of dogs during my time both on a response team and later on as a detective. Different police dogs are trained to sniff out different scents such as blood, accelerants, human scent, drugs and so on. I'm a huge 'animal lover' especially of dogs and the job of a dog handler, without any doubt, is the other career path I would have chosen if I wasn't a homicide detective. I often still think about making a switch to the dogs.

My best time in uniform was when I was posted on the 'area car'. This was the fastest car on the response team, which engaged in pursuits and was the first to respond to urgent calls. The driver of the area car is always a highly trained advanced driver. I was posted as the operator for the area car for three months. The operator in any police response car takes calls, navigates and communicates with the dispatch centres via the radio and car computer to get all of the available information regarding the call they are attending. I absolutely loved being on the 'area car'. It was the thrill of the speed I guess, and also being first on scene to the urgent calls. Due to the speed it was sometimes a dangerous place to be and literally just a few weeks after I finished my posting on the car, the same driver crashed whilst responding to an urgent call and sustained severe back injuries. He has thankfully since fully recovered and is still a serving officer.

'For all the excitement and fun times I had in uniform, there were also the unpleasant jobs that simply had to be done. One such time which stands out to me, is a bit of stinky one. A man was under arrest in hospital having smuggled drugs into the country. He had swallowed several condoms full of cocaine, and not long after entering the UK, one of the condoms had burst inside his stomach. He ended up in A&E begging for medical assistance as he was in pain and believed he was going to die, as many in this situation often do. These drug couriers are generally desperate for money and so take the big risk for a quick reward. The swallowing technique is designed to defeat x-ray, canines and manual searches. The aim is to later successfully excrete the condoms, or similar receptacles, containing the cocaine. Anyway on this occasion, myself and a colleague, also a probationer, were posted to maintain a constant watch over the prisoner during his stay in hospital. However, later on came the dreaded task of sifting through his runny, yellow excrement to retrieve the condoms and their contents, which would be subsequently used as evidence. One of us had to do it and my colleague would not entertain the idea for even two seconds, and flat out refused to do it. It fell to me to do the deed. So after the hospital administered him with strong laxatives, and with my mask, gloves and a big pair of tweezers in hand, I began the disgusting retrieval from the commode. After what seemed like a smelly eternity, I found them all. I cannot now, however, look at a chicken korma without having flash-backs!

I didn't plan on leaving uniform as quickly as I did. However, just a few weeks after coming off the area car I got posted to the CPU (Case Progression Unit) office on a ten week attachment. The CPU deals with prisoners arrested for minor crimes by the uniformed officers. It entails interviewing them in custody, liaising with the CPS (Crown Prosecution Service) and getting case papers ready for court if the suspect is charged. Most probationers on my borough did an attachment to the CPU during the two year probation period, but normally afterwards returned to their respective response teams. During my time there, however, applications for the 'trainee detective constable' (TDC) program came out. I was urged to apply for this by the CPU detective inspector as he saw my investigative potential. Just ten months service in uniform on the front line response teams is unheard of and I didn't think I would be accepted to become a trainee detective in CID so soon. I did enjoy being in uniform but I never felt that I had found my niche. I also felt that the investigation side of CID was more for me as I enjoyed finding the facts and piecing the puzzles together. So I applied for the TDC program, got accepted and never put my hat back on again!

CHAPTER 6

CID

The Criminal Investigation Department is the breeding ground for aspiring detectives and this was where I grew into myself and my career. Each of the thirty two boroughs of London policed by the Met has it's own CID. This is often split into different departments or squads such as robbery, burglary, CSU (community safety unit) which investigates domestic crimes, and the main CID office which investigates GBH, fraud, drugs offences, attempted murder and other serious offences.

I loved investigating crime in CID and even enjoyed the long hours. A typical day in CID involved attending and supervising crime scenes, seizing and viewing CCTV, visiting victims and witnesses, processing prisoners in custody and attending court. Each investigation became solely my own, so I had a lot of responsibility which I embraced one hundred percent. I was proud that I had made it into CID, especially so quickly and so I wanted to prove my worth.

An unnecessary barrier exists between uniformed officers and detectives which became more apparent to me when I joined the CID office. Uniformed officers are often referred to as 'lids' by detectives, whilst detectives are sometimes referred to as 'suits' or 'techos' by those in uniform.

The general consensus is that suits think lids are stupid and lids think suits are lazy. However, some of the most intelligent officers I've worked with have never left uniform and I have never met such hard working officers as those in the CID. Detectives in the CID units work unbelievably long hours – twenty plus hour stints are not uncommon when dealing with prisoners and crime scenes, only to then come back in and do it all over again the next day. On occasion a DC (detective constable) might not even get to go home at the end of the evening, but will instead nap on the office floor for two or three hours. This happened to me on a regular basis and I learned very quickly to keep an overnight kit bag under my desk at all times. The more it happened the more the overnight bag grew. It is a common sight to find camp beds and sleeping bags under detective's desks and in their lockers! Most police officers live a fair commute away from where they work and so at times it is madness to travel home just to grab a couple of hours in your own bed to do the commute back in again so soon after. This sleeping in the office is frowned upon by the bosses but needs must sometimes and unfortunately unlike the fire-brigade, the police do not provide sleeping quarters for their officers.

My most memorable moment in CID was successfully convicting a very cruel and heart-less woman of several artifice burglaries (also known as deception burglaries). She made a criminal career out of tricking her way into the homes of the elderly by posing to be a carer or a nurse. Once inside their homes she would distract them and steal money, handbags, jewellery and other items of value from them. She preyed on the vulnerability of elderly men and women who often would not realise they were victims of the thefts until hours, sometimes days after her visit.

I arrested, interviewed, charged and then compiled all the evidence against this despicable criminal to eventually secure her conviction at court. At no time did she ever express remorse or regret over what she did to her elderly victims, or over the negative effect she had on them afterwards. Being a victim of crime is not just about having property stolen and providing a statement to the police. It can be an emotionally scarring experience which can devastate the lives of many, since crime often affects not just the lives of the victims but their loved ones too. Many of her elderly victims were scared to open the front door again, most felt ashamed and foolish over having been tricked by her and one lady even died soon after following a heart attack, which may or may not have been related to her bad experience.

I received a commendation for convicting this woman but it meant little to me when I considered what she had done to the weak and vulnerable. She was one of the despicable people in society I was referring to when I spoke of meeting the worst of mankind in this job.

Another memorable experience I had in CID, although for an entirely different reason was during a big arrest operation to detain a violent gang of street robbers. This was a pre-planned operation to simultaneously arrest each gang member at their respective addresses. We were assisted by TSG (Territorial Support Group) officers who forced entry at each address at 5am and found, secured and arrested each suspect. Once they secured all occupants within and deemed each house as safe, they called us detectives in to commence the searches and take away our prisoners. I entered one of the addresses with two other detectives and went into the bedroom where a suspect had been found in bed. There was a bunk bed in this room and the suspect had been found on the top bunk bed and taken away by TSG. I began searching the room with my back to the now apparent empty bunk bed. After a short while searching, a movement in the lower bunk bed caught my eye and I pulled back the duvet to find a big-built seventeen year-old lad in the bed looking back at me. Next to his hand was a baseball bat. Luckily other colleagues were nearby to help me immediately restrain him. I will never know if he planned to stay under the covers and hope that he wouldn't be found or if he was waiting for the opportunity to attack me with the bat. I am glad I never got to found out which one of these it would have been. The TSG were blasted by my boss and the next morning I found a bunch of flowers on my desk with an apology note. This was a nice gesture by the officers, but more importantly to me, I know they will never make that mistake again!

The most frustrating aspect of policing is the hostility and blame culture which comes hand in hand when arrests are made and suspects are taken into custody. Obviously we expect and get volatile reactions from those detained but what always baffles and infuriates me are the reactions from most family members and some solicitors! The families and friends of those arrested can rarely see or admit that their loved one has committed the crime and that it was wrong of them to do so. On the odd occasion a parent of a street robber, for example, knows and openly admits that their child is breaking the law and asks the police for help to steer them back onto the right path. These precious few parents/guardians will do all they can to assist the police but then are hated by their own son or daughter. Those youths really frustrate me. The love and guidance from their own parents is there but they just reject it. When the suspect in custody is a juvenile, an appropriate adult is required to attend the police station and be with them during the booking-in procedure, interview and then release from custody into their care. The majority of these appropriate adults are parents/guardians or other family members. However sometimes the parents will put the phone down on the officer calling to ask them to come down to the station, whilst others slam the front door in our faces. These are the parents who have given up on their children after they have committed a number of offences. They just refuse to get involved and don't even want to know what crime they committed this time round.

I always feel sympathy toward those juveniles whose own parents have given up on them and refuse to guide and help them. However this sympathy is often short lived due to their intolerable lack of manners, respect toward me, my colleagues and a general disregard of the law.

A small part of me understands the hostility and sometimes aggressive behaviour from family members whose natural instinct is to protect their loved one. However what I will never understand is the rude, sometimes sarcastic behaviour from the solicitors who have no personal loyalty or bond to their clients in custody. They know the system, they know that the police have sufficient grounds to arrest and interview the suspects. They also know that the officers are simply carrying out their duty. However some solicitors who turn up in custody to represent those arrested can be so rude to the officers conducting the interviews. They are sometimes disruptive and speak to the police like we are the bad guys. They try their hardest sometimes to get these career criminals out of custody and back on the streets. I have always thought it and I still do, that I don't know how these solicitors do their job and can feel good or comfortable about it. It is as though they cannot imagine it was their own mother or sister who was robbed at knife-point or their frail old grandfather whose home was burgled during the night. Only once have I known a solicitor to arrive in custody to represent a suspect, and refuse to do so. On that occasion he recognised that the youth who was to be his client had robbed him just days before!

I once heard that a defence barrister whilst lecturing on a police training course was asked by an officer, "How do you sleep at night doing the job that you do?" they replied, "In a big house in a big comfy bed."

No greater honour will ever be bestowed
on an officer, or a more
profound duty imposed on him, than
when he is entrusted with
the investigation of the death of a
human being. It is his duty to
find the facts, regardless of colour
or creed, without prejudice,
and to let no power on earth deter
him from presenting these
facts to the court without regard to personality.

Anonymous

CHAPTER 7

Murder Most Horrid –
The Homicide Squad

After four years in CID I moved into homicide. It was quite difficult to get accepted into the murder squad then, so I was very proud.

The Homicide Command is the place to be for substantive experienced detectives. I personally felt like I had succeeded in the police when I made it in. The majority of detectives get in by recommendation from a higher ranking officer. I know I have a certain Detective Chief Inspector to thank for my success in joining the murder squad.

I joined a MIT (murder investigation team) based in central London, and have there had so far, the best time of my career.

I have worked on some amazing and unforgettable cases and spent a lot of time at The Old Bailey court house where I helped convict many of atrocious and horrific murders.

I was part of a team who convicted a child killer nearly thirty years after he brutally killed two young girls and their mother.

I played a pivotal role in convicting a four-man gang for the murder of an unarmed teenager.

I have been filmed by a BBC crew for a television documentary and I have also asked the public for their assistance during a live televised appeal on Crimewatch.

Homicide squads work differently to borough CID offices. No crime is investigated by one sole officer, since the work involved is of a much greater scale. When a murder investigation breaks, the entire team to which it is initially delegated, gets involved. This later gets scaled down to a smaller team within, consisting of core roles.

The core roles for each murder investigation consist of:

Family Liaison Officer (FLO)

CCTV Officer

Telephones Officer

House to House Officer

Witnesses Officer

Disclosure Officer

Exhibits Officer.

These roles are all undertaken by detective constables. The investigation in it's entirety is co-ordinated and managed by the Senior Investigating Officer (the SIO – the detective chief inspector (DCI) who is the highest ranking officer on that team). Answering directly to the DCI is the Investigating Officer (I/O – a detective inspector) and also the Case Officer (C/O – a detective sergeant)

Other detective constables who are not given a core role on the team get tasked to conduct research, visit witnesses, take statements, conduct arrest enquiries, assist with scene searches and so on. The team will then work on that investigation collecting the evidence and building a case against the defendant so it is water-tight ready for trial at court, months and months later.

I have resumed responsibility of the majority of the above listed roles for a DC, but most frequently of all I have taken on the role of Exhibits Officer for which I am now very well qualified and experienced.

The role of an exhibits officer is by far the busiest and most demanding role in any murder investigation.

I often take on this role which is integral in any homicide investigation on the team. I assess and process crime scenes with the Crime Scene Manager (CSM) and scientists. I attend the forensic strategy meetings and submit significant exhibits to the laboratory for forensic examination. It is also my responsibility to seize, package, record and store all exhibits correctly and efficiently. An exhibit is an object which is of potential relevance to an investigation, and therefore seized by the police. This can range from a bullet fired from a gun and later found at the scene of a shooting, a mobile telephone seized from a suspect in police custody or a financial document found at an address which has been searched following an arrest there.

I also attend scenes with the trained police search teams and decide if I want items found by them seized or not based on their relevance to the case. I will take possession of all items found by the search teams (sometimes car loads) and they become further exhibits to consider for examination and prioritisation.

It is also my responsibility to attend post mortems and seize exhibits from the deceased and complete a post mortem report. Prior to the post-mortem I will have wrapped the deceased in a body bag or body sheet at the scene.

As the exhibits officer I also work alongside the Graphic Design Studio at New Scotland Yard to produce a graphical presentation of the evidence (usually maps, plans and photographs of scenes and exhibits) which is referred to throughout the trial by the prosecution counsel.

It is also my responsibility to input all of the exhibits data onto the HOLMES system (a national database for homicide and other serious crime investigations) and ensure that it is updated accordingly with movements and submissions.

The HOLMES database which stands for the Home Office Large Major Enquiry System is a computer system used to store and cross-reference information on all national homicide and other serious and complex investigations in an organised manner. It was brought into effect following the failings of the Yorkshire Ripper investigation in the 1970s and early 1980s.

The problem encountered on that case was the huge quantity of information collected (approximately forty tons of paper). It was impossible for the investigating officers to gain a complete view of all the gathered evidence and information as a whole. The backlog of the unprocessed information resulted in the failure to connect vital pieces of related information. This major fault in the enquiry allowed Peter Sutcliffe to slip through the net as the evidence and information surrounding him was not married up and cross-referenced properly. Had a system such as the HOLMES been in effect at that time Sutcliffe would have been arrested, charged and convicted earlier than he eventually was. This also in turn would have prevented a number of the later killings being committed by the infamous serial killer.

Worn with pride

The Metropolitan Police crest on a Central
London Police Station building

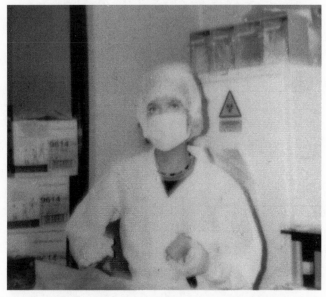

All suited up!.....my forensic science days in the laboratory

Chapter 2 – 'How Did It All Happen?'

Training days at Hendon with my revision
notes plastered around the room!

Chapter 3 – 'London Calling'

My passing out day with a proud mom and
under the watchful eye of Sir Robert Peel!

Chapter 3 – 'London Calling'

The essentials during my uniform days walking 'the beat'

Chapter 4 – 'In Uniform'

My desk on live TV during Crimewatch!

The world of an exhibits officer!

Chapter 7 - 'Murder Most Horrid'

A detective is interviewed by the press outside
the world famous New Scotland Yard

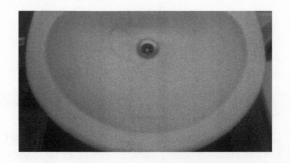

The before and after effect of Luminol showing
traces of blood present in a cleaned-up sink

Chapter 8 - 'Blood And Gore'

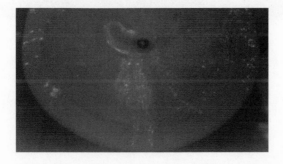

My commendations & medals

Chapter 13 – 'A Mother's Pride'

Chapter 8

Blood And Gore

This chapter comes with a warning. The squeamish among you may want to skip it!

I have witnessed some truly bloody and gory things as a police officer. I have seen victims who have died from horrific injuries in some of the saddest of circumstances. I have seen a variety of methods used to commit murder and unfortunately too, that of suicide. I have seen a victim who had sustained fifty seven stab wounds all over his body. Another was suffocated to death with a plastic bag by her own husband and was then left decomposing on the bathroom floor for days. The shock and desperation could still be seen in her eyes as she lay on the floor, her life extinct. I have seen bodies which have burnt to death, drowned, fallen from great heights, crushed by cars, ripped apart by trains and sadly bodies of those who have hanged, overdosed or stabbed themselves to death.

I attended one scene where a man had stabbed his two friends to death following an argument and was thought to have fled the house afterwards. The room was preserved by police and the scene examination had started when the suspect was found hiding inside the bed, underneath the mattress, below where one of the victims lay dead. After killing his friends he slashed his own wrists. He also cut through the material around the bottom of the bed where he then crawled in and remained for two days, slowly bleeding. He was discovered barely alive in his own blood, faeces, urine and also the blood of the victims which had seeped through the mattress.

Another dead body was so badly decomposed that the rotting flesh and body fluids had seeped through the floor beneath and through the ceiling in the room below. I had to package and remove this maggot-infested body, with it falling apart in my hands. The stench was unforgettable.

A man with mental health issues plunged an axe into a stranger's head during an unprovoked attack in a park in North London. As the night duty homicide on-call unit, I attended the scene in the middle of the night and saw small parts of his skull on the floor. The victim's head injuries were so bad that his brain was visible after he was struck several times with the axe. Amazingly, after lengthy rehabilitation he walks and talks again today. Even more bizarrley his attacker returned to the scene not long after the attack, with the bloody axe still in his hand! He was over-powered by the uniform officers on the cordon, was arrested and later pleaded guilty to attempted murder. He later received an order to remain in a psychiatric hospital.

The majority of murder scenes as you can imagine involve a lot of blood. Luminol is a chemical used in such scenes to determine the presence of blood where it has been cleaned up or not so visible to the naked eye. Most people are aware of luminol since it is often used in crime scene shows on television. Luminol is a versatile chemical which exhibits a striking green/blue glow when mixed with the iron found in heamaglobin in blood. It is sprayed across areas such as floors and walls, and the luminol glows where the blood is present. This is most effective in a darkened room. The glow only lasts for less than a minute but is recorded by photography. This techinique is especially useful in scenes which have been cleaned up by assaillants, or by those assisting them.

I once investigated a horrific case where an elderly female suffered unbelievable injuries following sexual abuse by a family member. She was vaginally and anally penetrated so deep by her attacker that some of her insides had ruptured during the assault, and had spilled onto the floor beneath her. She tragically died from the trauma. Her attacker, who was arrested at the scene, had cleaned up some of the blood in the room prior to police arrival. He denied the clean-up but the luminol proved otherwise. It was a terrible scene to examine.

Post-mortems are by far the strangest, most stomach-churning but fascinating experiences I have ever had during my time in the police. The literal translation of post-mortem from Latin is 'after death' and it is exactly that. It is the medical examination of a body to determine the cause of death.

When the circumstances of death are suspicious or unexplained, the examination becomes a 'special post-mortem' rather than the standard. The pathologist basically conducts a more intrusive autopsy which can last for several hours as they check every nook and cranny for signs of what happened.

I have attended many such autopsies as an observer behind a screen in the viewing gallery, but more often as an exhibits officer in the mortuary next to the body with the pathologist as he skillfully slices and dices! It is my job in the latter role to take from the pathologist samples and exhibits from the body as he examines and cuts away. Such samples include sections of liver for histology, vitreous humor (eye-ball fluid) taken for chemical analysis, blood samples, hair, nails, internal and external swabs, any clothing, bullets and other foreign objects inside or on the body. A photographer is also present during the examination to take images of the body in all stages during the process. I am used to the bodies being cut open with sharp scalpels, the ribs being cracked open and pulled apart. I don't even blink when the internal organs are pulled out and piled up inside a big bowl for weighing. I'm even unaffected by the sound of the circular chainsaw as the mortuary assistant saws through the top of the skull to remove the brain, which is then sliced through like a loaf of bread. But what gets me every time is when the skin is pulled back from the neck over the face. The skin from the face is then left pulled back like the inside of a mask and remains hanging off the back of the skull while the pathologist examines the exposed face under the skin for marks, breaks and other injuries. After he has completed his examination of the head the mask of skin is pulled back down over the face as if it never left. The photographer takes very clear images of all of this as it happens and I know of a quite few 'seasoned' murder detectives who cannot even look at such pictures.

A very experienced and competent exhibits officer I know who had 'seen it all' and even assisted in the London tube bombings scenes attended a particularly grim post-mortem once. Due to the over-powering stench coming from the body he threw up in his mask. Out of pride and the mentality of being an 'old sweat' he poured the sick into the neck of his body suit where it then dripped down and remained throughout the remainder of the examination. Nobody in the room knew about this at the time and it was only years later he saw the funny side of it and confessed!

The mortuary assistant not only has the brutal job of sawing through a skull to then remove the brain, but they also sew the body back up from the groin to the neck after the pathologist has finished his examination. They take to it as if they are darning an old sock, only with a slightly bigger needle & thread! They also clean the room of all the blood & mess following each autopsy, making it ready for the next one. It may not surprise you that mortuary assistants always strike me as being slightly odd characters.

In one case my team investigated a male who had been fatally stabbed and the murder weapon, a kitchen knife, was found with the tip of its blade missing. An X-ray team was brought into the autopsy room in an attempt to find the tip of the blade in the body. It was a potential theory at that time that during the stabbing the knife blade had hit a bone with such force that the tip had broken off inside the body. The X-ray failed to find the blade tip inside the corpse. However, an injury to one of the shoulders displayed 'grooves' from the knife which had been made during the stabbing. This shoulder was therefore cut out of the body and handed to the exhibits officer (my colleague) to package and later submit for a 'mechanical fit' also known as a 'physical fit' with the knife found at the scene.

The human body can change dramatically after death. So much so that we have to sometimes advise loved ones not to view the body, which many want to do in order to say goodbye and for their own closure.

One such body was found in the river Thames and had bloated so much that the man looked twice his usual size and was unrecognisable. A dead body can bloat on land or on water due to the presence of bacteria which is normally regulated by the immune system during life. However when we die these bacteria multiply quickly eating away at the body, which produces gas, which then bloats the body.

A female was suffocated to death and was found days later. Due to the warm conditions where she lay, decomposition was rapid and rife. On the mortuary table this once young white woman now resembled a black bloated man. From seeing the photographs of her before she died it was difficult to comprehend that the corpse in front of us was the same person.

Livor mortis, or lividity, is the gravitational settling of blood, post-death causing a purplish red discoloration of the skin. The time of and position of the body when death occurs are both often determined and assisted by livor mortis. For example, if the deceased is discovered lying face down but the blood pooling is present on the back, the body has most probably been moved from it's original face-up position.

The smell from a post-mortem or autopsy is a very distinctive and unforgettable one. It stays with you long after you have left the mortuary. It gets up your nose and it stays there for quite some time. Unlike the movies there is no paste to rub under your nose to disguise it. I think we may used to have done such a thing, but it is now thought that such ointments open up the airways and therefore can enhance the stench.

The one type of post-mortem I have had the fortune of not yet experiencing, but im sure I will in the future, is that of a baby or a child. Officers who have, some of them parents, describe it as heart-breaking and most distressing for all involved.

As an exhibits officer I am also further trained in Disaster Victim Identification (DVI).

DVI trained officers are those who attend major critical incidents or disasters at home or overseas, like the Tsnunami, 9/11 and the Bali bombings. The officer's role is to identify, package and preserve body parts. The Metropolitan Police Service has paved the way for DVI techniques and procedures and have trained many international agencies who have adopted this single universal protocol.

I know officers who helped out in the Tsnuami and describe it as the most harrowing and heart-breaking experience they have ever had. This was because of the volume of human life lost, the devastation the Tsnumai left behind, but also because of the lack of preparation, infrastructure and organisation out there. A lot has been learned since then.

I am now on this list of DVI trained officers and ready to travel when, not if, the next global disaster happens.

CHAPTER 9

The Old Bailey

The Central Criminal Court is based off Ludgate Hill near St Paul's Cathedral in the City of London.

It is universally known as the Old Bailey and is probably the most famous criminal court in the world.

Most homicide investigations within London go to trial at the Old Bailey. The most humble and rewarding times of my career have been whilst inside this prestigious court house. All the effort, long hours, lack of sleep and personal sacrifices made getting a murder investigation to court all seem worth it the moment I walk into the Old Bailey, and even more so when I hear the word 'Guilty'.

Many infamous defendants who have stood in the dock within this court house have included Dr Crippen, the Kray Twins, Lord Haw-Haw and the Yorkshire Ripper. All have risen to the court usher's instructions of "silence and be upstanding" only later to have heard the judge's stern command "take him down" after the jury foreman delivered a guilty verdict.

It is estimated that the collective time served by all of the defendants found guilty within these legendary walls is tens of thousands of years.

From the numerous homicide investigations I have taken to court, three stand out as ones I am particularly proud to have worked on.

Cold Case - Child Killer

For nearly twenty eight years Tony Dyce got away with the horrific triple murder of a mother and her two young children. He was twenty six years of age when he raped and killed a young mother in her home after following her back there from a nightclub in the summer of 1982. He then stabbed her nine year-old daughter to death and drowned her seven year-old daughter in the bath. The horrific scene was found two days later by the children's grandmother and her third grand-daughter who was lucky enough to be staying with her at the time. In 2009 during a case review Dyce's DNA was matched to a significant scene sample and he was arrested. Confronted with this evidence, Dyce denied the murders but he however was found guilty by the jury for all three murders on December 17th 2010 at the Old Bailey. He was sentenced to life imprisonment with no chance of parole.

This case struck many chords with me both professionally and emotionally for several reasons:

Dyce had not only gotten away with this abhorrent murder for close to three decades, but showed no remorse upon his arrest, during trial or upon being sentenced.

The two young girls were not only found dead by their own grandmother, but they were discovered dumped on top of each other in the bath tub sumerged in water. The chilling photographic images of the girls in the tub affected all the officers working on this case.

The surviving half-sister of the two murdered young girls was just four years old when she and her grandmother found the dead bodies in 1982. She is now a grown woman who has had no choice but to live her life without the love and support of her mother and sisters due to the evil that is Wilbert Anthony Dyce.

It is always nerve-racking awaiting any verdict at court, but this one in particular made me feel sick to my stomach. I did not want to let down the daughter/sister who had been sat in tears at the back of the court everyday though the long trial. I did not want Dyce set free to walk the streets of London again.

Dyce attempted suicide in his cell that evening after being sentenced. He was saved by the wardens on duty at that time and still lives and breathes today.

Murder For Gain

A truly shocking and terribly sad murder was that of a ninety one year-old man killed by a woman who battered him to death with a wine bottle in his own home. She killed the old man for the money he had in his coat pocket, since she was a desperate drug user and alcoholic. She quite literally, as we found out, would do whatever it took to get money to fund her habits.

The victim sustained horrific head injuries and was found covered in blood sitting on his bed, by his son. He later died in hospital. The scene in the victim's bedroom was truly awful since the walls and ceiling were splattered with large amounts of the poor old man's blood.

His killer was tried at the Old Bailey in 2011, and was convicted and sentenced to at least 30 years in prison.

On sentencing, the judge said to her "What is truly shocking is the brutality of what you did. It may be that you will never be released and may die in prison"

The one good thing to come out of that trial was the victim's family's faith and trust in the police. They were overwhelmed by the professionalism and dedication of the investigation team, and also the support received throughout the enquiry and the trial. This has since inspired the victim's grandson to become a police officer with the ultimate intention of joining a murder investigation team.

Torturous Revenge

A jealous and bitter man tortured a love rival to death with a hot poker for sleeping with his girlfriend. The victim was also beaten, stamped on until his skull fractured and had his kneecaps broken. He was also burned with boiling syrup. The killer was assisted by another during the torture whilst two others stood by and watched it happen. None of them at any time called for the police or an ambulance.

Audio from the horrific attack was taped on a phone by an engineer working inside the building, outside the flat. The victim was heard on the recording groaning and pleading whilst being shouted at, beaten and humiliated. This recording was listened to over and over by my colleagues and I during the investigation as it was a vital piece of evidence. During this recording of the attack, music by 'Blondie' was playing in the background. I can no longer listen to a particular track by the band without also hearing the victim's screams. I used to really like Blondie.

The killer later bragged to friends that he planned to chop up the body and throw the pieces in the Thames. After a five week trial he and one other were convicted of murder and sentenced to life.

Upon sentencing the judge said "Anyone who listened to the evidence in this case could come to no other conclusion than that this was a brutal and callous murder. Anyone who heard that tape will be affected by it for years to come."

Butchered Officers

One awful morning in 2012 four uniformed police
officers became the victims of a bloody attack inside
a butcher's shop in Kingsbury, North-West London.
Several 999 calls had been made regarding a man
walking down the high street holding a bottle of
alcohol, shouting at passers-by and ranting at the sky.
The attending officers approached him and he ran into
a shop where he grabbed tins of food which he threw at
the officers and their vehicle, smashing the windscreen.

Further units were called to assist, but before the officers
could detain him he ran into a butchers shop and grabbed
a twelve inch long knife from behind the counter. He
lashed out with the knife at the police officers in front
of terrified staff and customers. One officer was knifed
in the stomach and later during surgery had a section
of intestine removed. He suffered "unspeakable pain"
and later said he thought he was going to die. Another
officer who was stabbed in the face and arm, when he
went to help his colleague, was left with a prominent
scar on his face. A third officer was stabbed deep in his
leg whilst a fourth officer sustained a broken hand.

I attended Kingsbury but was not the exhibits officer on
this occasion so I did not attend the actual scene inside

the butcher's shop. However, a close colleague of mine who did assist in the examination of the scene told me of a complete 'blood-bath' and how the floor was covered in blood and meat fat making it very slippery. It was difficult for him to maintain his footing whilst working in there sealing and packaging the various sharp knives and cleavers. Imagine the fear the officers must have gone through as they slipped and slid across the floor as they came under attack from a twelve inch blade. Even the meat on display was covered in human blood, and he described it as your classic horror movie scene, and a sight he will never forget. My role in this case was interviewing witnesses and conducting 'house to house' enquiries. Many local residents and shop owners were in shock over the events. One woman I spoke to was hugely distressed as she was in the shop when the man ran inside. He pushed her against the wall but she managed to run out, luckily for her.

The defendant who suffered from paranoid schizophrenia was later found guilty on two counts of attempted murder, grievous bodily harm and actual bodily harm. It is the many unsung heroes such as these wounded officers for whom I have written this book.

Chapter 10

Women In The Work Place & Sexism?

As a female in the police I often get asked how do I find it working in a male dominated environment. I don't know the exact figures to quote here but the percentage of female officers within the police is no doubt constantly increasing and is significantly higher than it was ten or even five years ago.

The Met certainly doesn't feel massively dominated by men, like it was not so long ago, but they remain greater in numbers and it does still does feel at times like a 'man's world'. The days of the newly recruited WPC being bent over a desk and having her behind stamped may be a thing of the past but such things are not forgotten. There are still echoes of such playful banter running through the Met. I think that's all it is, playful banter, as do most, but a small minority do get offended....and an even smaller minority like to think they do.

For all the harmless banter, there are obviously those who do still believe women should not be in the police. As recently as earlier this year in 2014 a well respected and experienced male officer voiced exactly that in the office and started a very heated debate. I was quite surprised that he vocalised his opinion on such a controversial subject in an open office.

An incident which involved me, and which I'm sure was more of a thoughtless oversight than outright sexism, was during a early morning arrest or 'spin' as it's often called. The entire team of about twenty detectives was briefed early one morning to attend an address in London where a murder suspect was known to be residing. The five female officers on duty that day all got posted together in the same vehicle and were tasked to remain down the street, out of sight and at the furthest point away from the target address. We were referred to (in jest) as 'Lipstick-One' for the remainder of that day and were asked (again in jest) to go get coffees for the boys. I later learned that the sergeant who arranged that set-up was later taken aside and given an earful from the DI (Detective Inspector)...a female DI nonetheless.

Other than that small incident, which is more laughable than offensive, I have never been the victim of sexism in the work place although I have heard a handful of accusations and arguments surrounding it.

I once for a long period of time worked with a number of female DCs who felt held back and ignored by a particular male sergeant. He was very much a 'Jack The Lad' type character and always surrounded himself with male colleagues both inside and outside work. He wasn't known for providing many work opportunities for the female officers and nearly always took the male DCs out with him on the 'golden nugget' leads and enquiries. This sergeant was in no doubt an excellent detective and the most enthusiastic one I have ever worked with. He liked to have the best detectives working alongside him at all times and was known to 'cherry-pick' his team. Because of his blatant dismissal of certain officers I was actually at times quite humbled that he often picked me to be on his team. I also socialised with him and the other male officers, and so therefore sometimes felt as the 'go between' of this obvious sex divide, since I was friends with the female officers too. I remain good friends with both some of the girls and the lads today. I just hope that they never felt any bitterness toward me because of my acceptance by the boys. I don't think they did. I wasn't completely naive, and was aware that there was a minor element of sexism from that male officer who was at times very judgemental and unfair towards the female officers. However, I also thought that the female DCs perhaps didn't always push themselves as hard as the male DCs did. Their argument was that they were never given the opportunities to do so... and so the viscious circle went round and round.

The male DCs generally worked longer days and volunteered to stay on at work when needed more than the women generally did. I'm not saying the girls didn't work hard, they just had a greater work-life balance which looking back on now, I envy. I sometimes wish I had balanced my life better instead of pouring every ounce of my energy into work. Having said that, had I not devoted so much time and energy to work I would also have been frowned upon by certain male colleagues like the other girls were and possibly then not had the opportunities and experiences that I have had.

When I joined this team it was approximately 90% male dominated. I must say during that time the jobs got done, there were no tears or tantrums at work and few fall outs. Within two years a number of female officers had joined the team and the dynamics changed dramatically.

Who am I to say if it was the men reacting negatively to an influx of women before giving them the chance to prove themselves, or whether it was the women not performing to an expected certain standard.

All I know is that the team was never the same again.

One of the best detectives I have ever worked with was a female Detective Inspector. She was so switched on, knew the cases inside out and worked long long days. She always looked glamorous and professional, and I was inspired by her, as were the majority of the officers on the team. I never told her so but she influenced me to keep knuckling down and strive to be as great at my job as any of my male peers.

I quote her during a police interview which focused on recognising women in the police, when she said "keep your femininity, but be one of the boys!"

CHAPTER 11

Public Perception

Nobody I meet for the first time ever guesses what I do for a living. Most are shocked when I tell them. A few simply don't believe me.

I have been told on a couple of occasions that I look like I should be a hairdresser. I have no idea why this is …..I don't even know the first thing about hair-dressing!

An occasional and very flattering response "but you're too pretty to be a police officer" is also quite annoying, and with time, has worn thin.

I know that some people out there are of the opinion that women should not be in the police and that it is a job for a man.

On one occasion, when I was still in uniform, I was stood on a crime scene cordon in south London when an elderly female approached me and asked me if I was filming. She thought I was an actress from the popular police TV show, The Bill (the filming studios were local). She appeared disappointed and sceptical when I explained more than once that I was a real police officer on duty. She was very sweet and it made me smile, but once again the public's perception of me was dictated by my sex and my appearance.

A trip to New York provoked a similar reaction. I was there in 2010 with my then husband and we decided to visit a police station. It was not too far from Times Square and was surprisingly quiet on that evening. A male officer on the front office desk greeted us as we walked in. We explained that we were both police officers from London and that we just wanted to visit a local police station there in New York and look around. His response was this - he pointed to my husband and said "well yeah, you're a cop". He then pointed to me and said "you're a cop???" He didn't believe that I was an officer too because he said that I didn't look like one! After I convinced him that I was indeed too a police officer he kindly showed us round the building, which was a nice surprise! I don't know what I expected to see in that New York police station but it was so surprisingly similar to a typical London police station, from the parade room to the custody suite. The only main obvious difference I could see from my short time there was that all the officers were armed.

I have also had mixed responses from those on the other side of the law. I recall being faced with an extremely verbally abusive mother whose sixteen year old son I had just arrested for possessing a loaded handgun and a huge batch of cannabis. It was a dirty unkempt house which stank of that all-too familiar pungent cannabis smell. There was no doubt that she knew what he had in his room and that he was dealing from the family home. As I escorted her son from the house she continued to verbally abuse me and even questioned MY ability to ever be a good mother. She also threatened me that I would get what was coming to me. I just took this as another empty threat from a mother unable to see the reality of what her son was mixed up in. In her frustration she saw to blame the police, a common feeling among parents I soon came to realise.

On another occasion a middle aged man, whom my male partner had just arrested for assaulting his wife, screamed that he would find my mother and then rape the both of us. Sometimes it beggars belief what we hear but one has to remain professional at the worst of times and ignore such threats and atrocities. I have never once taken a threat personally. I would not be in the job still had I ever done so. You just have to remind yourself that such reactions are aimed at the uniform and the organisation.

The worst reaction I had because of my sex in the police was back in 2004 when I was again still in uniform. This was the one and only time I have ever been truly in fear of my life whilst at work. I was posted in a response car on a night duty shift in south London and was partnered with another female who was in her late fifties and was very close to retirement. There was no doubt she knew how to do her job and knew the law inside out, but I never felt entirely comfortable posted with her on a night shift in a dangerous part of London. I always thought that female officers on a response team should be paired up with male officers during the night shifts. To me that is not sexism, it is common sense. Men are generally stronger and faster than women, and that is a fact. As a female officer you can never anticipate that moment when you need a male colleague at your side.

That time for me came following a call from local residents complaining about a group of youths dealing drugs on a housing estate. The call came through on the car radio and being the closest unit we accepted it and drove to the estate. I half expected to see kids running as we arrived on scene and thought I might get a foot chase, always good fun. However I immediately saw a group of seven or eight young men. They were big and looked very intimidating. They did not look one bit bothered or concerned upon seeing two female officers get out of the police car. My partner called for extra units on her radio as we walked toward the men. One of the group walked straight towards me stopping inches from me, with his face almost touching mine. With his eyes bulging in anger he screamed at me to "fuck off!" I told him to stop where he was and asked him to show me what he had in his hands. He shouted at me again and lurched forward as if to hit me. The other men had grouped around us by this point and I had no idea where my partner was as I was surrounded. All I could think was that I was done for. They all towered over me in height and I felt like a helpless little girl. The main one lurched toward me. I think I even closed my eyes and waited for the impact. The greatest sight and sound you can hope for in a situation like that is that of the 'blues and twos' and that miraculously for me is what happened. A solo male officer from my team came flying around the corner onto the estate in his marked car with sirens and lights going. He got out the car and ran towards us whilst shouting down the radio. Mark my words when I say that this group of thugs, who moments before surrounded me, took one look at my male colleague and legged it. Quite literally.

Do you think they would have done a runner had it been a third female officer who turned up?

I don't.

Do you think they would have remained there as they did when we initially arrived, had one, or both of us, been a male officer?

I don't.

I'm not sure which emotion was more rife in me after they disappeared. Was I more relieved and thankful for the arrival of my male colleague? Was I more angry that the situation had been able to happen at all? Or was it that I was so stunned by the total disregard of the police uniform, and even more so because it was a woman wearing it.

The absolute opposite of the effect a woman in uniform can have happened only weeks after this episode. Two patrol cars arrived at a flat following major sounds of a disturbance. Inside was an extremely irate and hostile male who was throwing things, lashing out and screaming. He would not calm down for the male officers who were desperately trying to reason with him. I cannot recall what exact words I used but within moments of speaking with him, I managed to get this same man calmly sat on the floor apologising for his behaviour and crying to me for help. I remember him saying "god bless you darling". It seemed to me all he needed was a 'woman's touch'.

Again I don't think this is me making a sexist remark here. We each have our place at work just as we do in everyday life. A husband may take the bins out, mow the lawn and tile the bathroom. A wife may do the laundry, spring clean the house and bathe the children. In any situation we all have our own strengths and weaknesses and that is no different in the police. There are of course exceptions to the standard rule, as always, but generally men are better in a physical conflict as they are evolutionary stronger and quicker than women. This is not sexism, it is fact, and therefore also common sense.

I have never been offended when the men go to the front of the group when we force a door in during a 'raid' or when a physical fight is inevitable. It is an instinctive and protective trait for them to do so. At just five feet, six inches tall and weighing nine stone it would be senseless and foolish of me to restrain a violent man when my taller, heavier and stronger male colleagues are at my side.

I was on one occasion tasked with dealing with a vulnerable and emotionally unstable female witness during a homicide investigation. It fell to me to obtain an account from her, take her to hospital, re-house her and quite literally 'babysit' her and her young child since a fellow male colleague could simply not cope or engage with her. I was chosen out of the dozen or so of us on duty that day to deal with her since I was the only female officer there. I was a little annoyed initially by this delegation, but also not surprised. As it turned out it was probably was the wisest decision to task me with the woman since she had several personal issues with men, and so she most probably responded better to me than she would have with a male officer. I also believe I obtained a better evidential witness account from her by gaining her trust and a 'woman to woman' rapport and understanding. She even told me that the male officer who was with her the day before was an idiot! I ended up spending several days with her since she needed to be mentally assessed, re-housed to another city, and I also had to ensure her baby was safe and healthy. Although many of the male officers in my team are brilliant detectives, I doubt any of them would have coped as well or communicated as well as I did with her. This is another example of the differences in ability, strength and natural instinct between the two sexes, and the necessity of these differences within the police service.

Chapter 12

Home-Life & Family

Looking round my office in the homicide squad one day, a friend and I between us counted how many of us were divorced or separated. Out of the twenty officers we counted thirteen. Out of those thirteen, eleven of these break-ups had occurred during their time in that office. A huge factor in these relationship break downs was in no doubt due to the hours worked and therefore the lack of time spent at home with loved ones. A great relationship is almost always sacrificed because of 'The Job'. I'm fairly confident when I say a huge percentage of Metropolitan police officers have divorced their partners during their time in service.

As you can imagine a lot of relationships are formed within the police service due to the long hours worked with fellow colleagues and the experiences we officers go through together.

I met my husband at work when we both worked in CID together. He proposed to me within ten months of dating. Within another ten months we were married. We are now though, after six years of marriage, unfortunately in the process of divorcing. All marriages have their own problems and issues but our ultimate problem was 'The Job'. He worked long hours, I worked longer hours and we rarely had quality time together. He wanted me to start a family from our first year together and yet six years in, I still wasn't ready. He believed my priority was 'The Job' over everything else, and he was most probably right.

None of the eleven women on my team in homicide had children and all of them were over thirty years of age. Of the men at least two thirds had children. I strongly believe that it is both rare and difficult to excel as a full-time police officer and a mother at the same time in the Met. For the men it rarely makes any difference. They still do both jobs since, although time has moved on, their wives are often full time house mums, part-time workers or just not police officers! Those mothers who are police officers are often part-time. For those few who are both mothers and full-time police officers I take my hat off to you!

There is no doubt that the police maternity package is good, it really is. However after those six months at full pay, a female detective cannot return back to job she did in a squad and be as effective as she was before she became a mother. You simply cannot do this due to the working hours expected and the demands of the work. You make a choice, detective or mother. My choice was to remain a murder detective and at thirty eight years of age I am still no nearer to starting a family. With the majority of my close friends and female relatives all now with children I wonder did I make a huge mistake?

My sister has told me on more than one occasion that she envies my career. She has two wonderful sons and I can't help but envy her family life style. It is quite possibly something I may now never have for myself. My best friend who has been my life-long friend since birth, and is as dear to me as a sister, also has two sons. I adore her boys and although I don't get to spend nearly as much time as I would like with them, I consider them as family and along with my two nephews, are probably the closest I will ever get to having my own.

CHAPTER 13

A Mothers Pride

My mother, bless her, is so proud of what I do for a living that whenever she gets the chance she tells all exactly that. I am the youngest of three children, and even at the age of thirty eight she still refers to me as her 'baby'. A typical introduction from her to a friend or colleague would be "This is my baby. She's a homicide detective in London!" I then get bombarded with the same questions which I always get asked. "Don't you get scared?" "Do you see dead bodies?" "Do you carry a gun?" (which I don't) and then this is usually followed by "I don't know how you do your job. I couldn't do it!" I have actually been told just that before by a nurse, a social worker and even a paramedic! I don't know how they do their jobs! Horses for courses I guess.

These questions come up at most social events especially when meeting people for the first time. When they get wind of the fact that I am a police officer, and in homicide, the conversation always steers toward that. I politely answer questions but then try to change the topic. People are naturally drawn to what they believe to be the exciting and glamorous world of being a detective. I believe film and television has a lot to do with that, especially these days when you cannot turn the TV on without seeing an advert for a new 'cop' or 'crime scene investigation' show.

I don't tell my mum even half of what I deal with and face at work. She would have kittens if she knew!

I often dilute the details for her benefit since she would not sleep at night if she knew the reality of some of the situations I have found myself in over the years. She will indeed learn for the first time about some of my close calls and grisly dealings whilst reading this book!

Over the years I have missed several important family dinners, weddings and functions because of work commitments. I worked Christmas Day and Boxing Day last year, as I have done many years before, and so my mum arranged for an early Christmas celebration for all the family one week before at her house. We all travelled home to her for that weekend ready to enjoy the time together. That first night, however, during dinner and having only been home for just a few hours, I received orders to get back to London first thing in the morning to assist on a new investigation. This call ruined my dinner that night, and I was awake and out of the door by 5am the following morning. I worked incredibly long hours that weekend whilst my family were all together at home enjoying themselves and revelling in an early Christmas. I felt bad for my mum who loves to have her children and grandchildren around her, as any woman would at such a special time of the year. She was disappointed that I had to leave so soon and even got up at 5am to wave me off at the door. I felt really guilty driving away in the dark that morning, and then lonely on the quiet motorway back to London. My favourite Christmas song is 'Driving Home For Christmas' by Chris Rea and that came on the radio that lonely morning but sadly I was driving the wrong way.

It may come as no surprise that moments like those are when I ask myself "what am I doing this for?" and "how long can I keep on doing this?" Those thoughts however disappear from my mind the moment I reach London and again immerse myself into the despicable but exciting world of another horrific murder investigation.

Back for a moment to that common response "I couldn't do what you do" It does take a certain type of person to be a police officer. It is definitely not a career path for everyone, that's for sure. You need to be strong minded and hard-working, but also patient and understanding. I got those qualities from my mum. She is the most successful, hard-working and kind woman I know and I am very proud to be her "baby". I would not be a police officer today if it wasn't for the strengths I have inside of me, which I no doubt inherited from her. Growing up she was the perfect mother, and I even knew that at the time. Many of my friends wished they had parents like mine. My mum and my dad raised us in a very loving and fun home where we wanted for nothing. Mum was the best role model to all three of us kids and we have all grown up to be successful and strong-willed people.

She is a very caring and lovable woman and everybody who knows her loves her for her constant cheeriness and laughter. She lights up a room with her presence and I feel like that much loved child again whenever I'm back home and around her.

She is the glue which holds our family together and who we all flock home to between our busy schedules and hectic lives.

Chapter 14

Nasty Surprises

There have been many unpleasant surprises and shocks throughout my career as you would imagine. Some have been far worse than others and I have images in my head which will never be erased.

Being a police officer has given me an insight into the lives of others which I would otherwise be none the wiser of. Things which most people would find disturbing or strange can just be the way of life for others. Before I moved to London and before I became a police officer I lived in a pleasant bubble. I knew nothing of crime, poverty or of how violent and cruel life can be.

I wish at times that I had not experienced and seen certain things, but it comes with the territory! I am sure there will be plenty more nasty surprises to come.

The conditions in which some people choose to live life, at times astonishes and unfortunately disgusts me. I have seen numerous people living in needless squalor and mess. I have seen many such places, but the state of one house specifically remains in my mind. From the outside and to any passer-by it was a normal looking semi-detached house in a normal residential street which subsequently became a crime scene following a vicious assault on one of the occupiers. For no reason other than tardiness, the house was in such an awful and uninhabitable state that I could not believe adults had actually been residing there for many years and considered it as their home.

Each room was full of rubbish, rotten food and dirty dishes whilst the walls were caked in grease and cigarette-smoke stains. The carpets were also soaked with grease and grime, so much so that my feet would stick to the floor as I walked through the house. This was one of those rare occasions when as uncomfortable and hot as I was, I was glad to be wearing the police over-shoe protectors, a full forensic body suit, a face mask and two pairs of forensic gloves!

I was reluctant to move any of the piled-up rubbish around me for fear of it all falling down, but when I did carefully move anything I would discover flies, fleas, maggots and worse still, rats. When my partner and I stood still and kept quiet we could hear the insects and rats moving around. When I went home that night, having spent all day inside the house, I left my shoes outside the door and scrubbed them. I put my clothes straight into the washing machine and had a scorching hot shower during which I repeatedly washed my hair. I still felt itchy and dirty afterwards and I could still smell the stench from inside the house too. Such horrid smells tend to stay with you when you leave putrid crime scenes or mortuaries.

Another unpleasant memory is from when I saw a familiar face on the examination table during a post-mortem. A fellow colleague of mine who was a uniformed officer unfortunately took his own life a few years ago. I knew this man to say hello to daily at work but no more than that. He took his own life in a place which fell within the geographical remit of our CID, where I was based. A post-mortem was required and it fell to me to attend. Although I barely knew him, his face was very familiar and so it was a daunting experience to see someone you recognise being cut open and examined on a mortuary table. It was a shock to all his colleagues and friends that he ended his own life since he always appeared to be a happy and chatty person. As police officers we attend suicides all too often but you never expect it to happen to one of your own. I think we all forget that police officers are also human and too sometimes suffer the same emotional upsets, pressures and complexities which life throws at us. That officer is not the first to have taken his own life, and he unfortunately will not be the last.

As an exhibits officer, it is often necessary to wrap up a dead body in a body bag or a body sheet at the scene to forensically preserve it until the post-mortem examination, usually the following day.

I have wrapped up several bodies in my time and it is a sad and unpleasant experience due to injuries and the state of the corpses. However, one such experience has specifically remained with me for several reasons. With a colleague, I wrapped up the body of a murdered young male who had been stabbed multiple times. I had never seen so much blood in my career. It was literally dripping off the gurney and was like a scene from a horror film, and that was just the first shock. He was the youngest person I had ever prepared for a post-mortem and he looked even younger than his years as he lay in front of me, his life now completely extinct. As I moved and held him in place he felt like a little boy and all I could think about were his poor family, especially his mother. At this time his identity was unknown and the next morning near the scene I met one of his family members who was in tears holding his photo while asking me was this the dead boy found by police, as he was missing. I knew immediately that the boy in the photo was the same boy I had wrapped in a body bag, just hours prior. His identity had not been confirmed at this stage, but I knew instantly. I felt so extremely sad for them and for a moment completely lost for words.

One afternoon, two colleagues of mine were chasing after a male who had run from them during a standard 'stop and search' procedure. As they caught up with him, the man turned to face them and produced a bottle of liquid which he then threw at them. The bottle contained acid. Both officers were hit in the face with this acid which immediately began to burn through their skin. One of the two lads is now left with permanent scar down his face and the other nearly lost the sight in one of his eyes. Two female officers who had joined the foot-chase were stripped down to their underwear in the middle of the street, where they were immediately hosed down with water by other colleagues. This was in plain sight of all the public who had gathered there. That was a shocking day for all of us on duty, but most of all for the female officer in the control room who heard the chaos and panic for assistance coming from the police radios. She had to remain calm and make quick but correct decisions. That is a lot of pressure for anyone in that position when fellow officers are injured and urgently need assistance. On this occasion, however, for her it was a whole different ball game. One of the two male officers who had acid thrown in his face and which later left him permanently scarred, was her fiancé.

Police officers, especially those in uniform, are sometimes targeted by the dregs of society. A close friend of mine was patrolling through a housing estate with a colleague when a fridge was dropped from a top floor balcony above them. Luckily for them it landed just feet from them, in pieces. Both were left uninjured from that cowardly attack, and unfortunately those responsible got away with it since they were never identified.

A friend of mine was patrolling an area of North London with her partner when they found reason to pull over a car. One of the occupants of this car reacted by producing a handgun, and just like a scene from a Hollywood movie, shot at her and her partner. The officers pursued the car and managed to over-power and arrest the gunman. Both later received bravery awards for their actions that day.

For all of these awful moments and unpleasant experiences, I feel it is safe to say that I've pretty much seen or heard it all, and that nothing really shocks me anymore

Nothing really scares me anymore either......except for spiders but that's a whole other story!

CHAPTER 15

7/7

I don't really have much to say about the 7/7 terrorist attack in London.

We all know about the horror which took place and we have all seen the haunting images of the aftermath and the victims walking around the streets injured and dazed.

However, I wanted to acknowledge the incident in my book out of respect and a moral duty as a serving police officer in London.

When the tube bombings happened on 7th July 2005 I was working in the burglary squad at a police station in south London.

It was the first and only time since leaving uniform that I wished I had not left.

I remember the day clearly and felt useless since none of us detectives in my particular department were allowed to leave the police building. This was because we were not in uniform and also because we were awaiting instruction. So we remained inside the police building all day unable to do any regular work and whilst waiting to be tasked listened and watched the events unfold like the general public did. I wanted to be out there at any of the scenes across London helping the injured and my uniformed colleagues.

In 2005 I was neither an exhibits officer nor DVI trained as I was in the early stages of my detective career. Had I been, I more than likely would have been processing those scenes of horror and carnage across London. I later in my career worked alongside two highly skilled exhibits officers who worked in the underground bomb explosion scenes.

They have spoken of the terrible conditions down there; the heat, the sights, the smells and the eerie silence of the aftermath. Both however said that the most shocking and incomprehensible aspect of it all was that this awful attack on human life had happened not overseas, but at home, in London.

I was living at the time in Paddington section house (temporary housing for police officers above Paddington Police Station). Opposite to this station is Edgware Road tube station, which was one of the bomb explosion sites. I used to alternate my commute to work between cycling and taking the underground from Edgware Road. On that dreadful morning I cycled.

When I cycled back home that night I saw all the boarding up around the underground station and the police station. There was strangely odd and calm atmosphere and I wasn't sure what to feel.

CHAPTER 16

The Future

Ask any 'old sweat' about the current state of the Metropolitan Police Service and the majority will say "it's not like it used to be" or "I'm so glad I'm retiring soon". In the last year or two I have seen annual pay increments get frozen, pensions being changed for the worse, years of service being extended, free rail travel stopped, squads suddenly disbanded at the stroke of a pen and officers being relocated anywhere in London and expected to do any job with little or no choice over it, at the drop of a hat.

Officers in numbers are now transferring out of The Met to other forces or quitting the police entirely. Some are having break-downs or are off work with stress due to the volume of work, and the pressures and responsibilities that come with it. It is no longer a certainty that the police will remain a career for life for all who join, as it used to be.

As I write this, three officers have resigned within one week. That used to be unheard of.

It takes a very strong-willed person to stay in the Met in these modern times. Either that, or someone who is completely in love with 'The Job' and cannot entertain the idea of doing something else. These days it takes someone who can keep giving their all and not expect much back.…..except a guaranteed wage and a pension, albeit reduced.

I cannot tell you if I will still be in The Met in ten years time.

I cannot tell you whether I will be fed up of it all by then.

All I can say for sure is that I don't regret joining the police for one second. Looking back over my last decade fills me with pride and a sense of belonging.

Writing this book has caused me to weigh those positive feelings up against all the thoughts and realisations about how different my life, not only could, but would have been had I chosen different career.

Chapter 17

I Didn't Always Want To Be A Police Officer

I didn't always want be a police officer.

But what a life so far…..

In my service I have wrapped up dead bodies, searched the most horrific crime scenes and convicted killers at The Old Bailey.

I have arrested numerous offenders ranging from shop-lifters to murderers.

I have had lengthy foot-chases and high-speed vehicle pursuits.

I have been slapped, bitten, spat at and wrestled to the ground.

I have appeared on Crimewatch during a live televised appeal, and also interviewed by the BBC for a police documentary.

I have helped advise a Hollywood actress research her role as a police officer.

I have met the best of mankind but also the worst.

I have seen things the general public will never have the pleasure, or the horror of experiencing.

Being a police officer has brought out the best of my character but also the worst.

There are terrible images in my head which will never be erased.

I have sacrificed a marriage, possibly the chance of having children, and friendships with those who don't understand the life I lead and the hours I work.

I ask myself sometimes why I bother doing what I do.

Why don't I get a normal 'nine to five' job like most people?

My life simply is 'The Job'.

So after eleven years service & many more to go, I ask myself...

Would I do it all again?....

Probably.

CHAPTER 18

A Final Note

I read a blog recently online, and the officers among you may have also come across this yourselves. It was written by a fellow police officer, Nigel Thompsett. What he has written is so true, that as soon as I read it I knew I wanted to include it here in my book. Nigel has given me permission to include his blog in my book and I have chosen to use it here as a last thought. I consider it the perfect way to end this book as a means to highlight exactly how much police officers give everyday in the line of duty.

Since I joined the Police, way, way back then, I have learned
*   much and performed many, many roles.*
Some of them easy and some of them not so easy.

I have been:

a marriage guidance counsellor

an acting veterinary nurse,

a teacher,

a babysitter,

I've listened to advice from knowledgeable and experienced people,

I've also listened to advice from idiots and people who do not have a clue what they are talking about,

I've been an odd job man,

a translator,

a wrestler,

a boxer,

a fight referee,

a vehicle repair engineer,

a traffic controller,

a dog catcher,

a nightclub doorman,

a member of the sprint detention team,

a person who delivers unfortunate and unwanted bad news,

a person who sometimes delivers good news,

I have entered with a key, without a key through an open door and sometimes kicked or forced that door that prevents entry,

a writer of fact,

a listener of fiction,

I have been a cook,

an arbitrary decision maker,

a companion,

I have not told lies to cover someone else's backside,

I have been a friend,

a plan or map drawer,

a walking encyclopedia,

I have seen over-promotion for strategic credibility instead of policing credibility,

I have seen countless guidelines and recommendations ignored because it suits someone else's agenda,

I have been a good Samaritan,

a walking street-map,

a local information centre,

a medic,

an emergency plumber,

I have been spat at, punched, kicked, head butted, verbally abused, had things thrown at me or been threatened with a bladed instrument (formerly a knife),

I have seen many fine officers frustrated by those who appear to have forgotten that they were once a 24/7 police officer.

I have been a taxi-driver,

an unwanted guest,

a welcome guest,

a listening ear,

a mind reader,

I have walked many a whole night shift in the freezing night air, in the pouring rain or in the humid, sweltering muggy heat dressed in a uniform that was not suited to allow me to do some of the things I expected to come across,

I have been a surrogate and temporary parent,

I have been someone's worst nightmare,

I have been someone's saviour,

I have seen someone take their first breath as well as their last breath,

I have been a one man cordon,

I have experienced only a handful of very good senior officers,

I have been one of a small group against a far larger group,

I have been very, very, very patient, tolerant & understanding,

I have been considerate, restrained and hidden my true feelings,

I have been accused of being a liar,

I have saved a life,

I have failed to save a life,

I have seen and smelt death,

I have comforted and reassured,

I have always learnt from what I have done,

I have been an emergency fireman,

I have been the last person someone wanted to see as well as the first,

I have been loved, hated, admired and despised in varying amounts.

I have always tried my best,

I understand that those who police and those who manage/lead are fundamentally different because of the roles they do,

I have gone home at the end of my shift because my colleagues have been there with me,

I have been scared for my own safety,

I have acted without fear for my own safety but to protect others who are in fear themselves,

I have always been judged by those who do not do the same job, take the same risks or work under the same accountability as I,

I have listened to countless politicians talk about how they want to improve my role, how they need to show how I am accountable and how they want to make my job easier,

I have protected life and property,

I have the respect of my peers,

I have listened to countless senior management talk about how they are improving my role only for them to move on and the next in line change things to support their own career aims and not to support or complement the work done by their predecessor,

I have wasted far too much of my time and effort completing statistical information for other people to justify their own position or to show how well they are managing what I do, yet none of these people know me,

I have listened to countless senior management talk about how they are improving my role only for them to move on and the next in line change things to support their own career aims and not to support or complement the work done by their predecessor,

I have wasted far too much of my time and effort completing statistical information for other people to justify their own position or to show how well they are managing what I do, yet none of these people know me,

I have repeated the last two things because they have probably had the most negative effect on me during my service.

I have learned about tolerance, compassion, that there are a lot of nice people out there but still some people who have no social conscience and will burgle your house or even kill someone and not care one bit about doing so,

I have seen the victim not see justice all too often,

I have seen colleagues fail to get the recognition they deserve,

I have seen repeat offenders not get custodial sentences,

I have seen Policing become a brand to be promoted at every available opportunity, some of them totally inappropriate.

I have experienced poor vehicles because they are cheaper,

I have been subject to mileage restrictions because of targets,

I have been advised because I have not reported enough people or submitted enough admin for people to measure,

I have experienced death in many forms, from violent, unexpected and unpleasant to peaceful, calm and dignified,

I have led a varied and rewarding career.

Nigel Thompsett

"My sincere thanks to Nigel Thompsett for inspiring me with your blog, and allowing me to use it within my book"